Powerfully Perplexing

Presidential Profiles

Rod Martinez

Powerfully Perplexing

Presidential Profiles

Illustrated by Cat Purcell

Histria Kids

Las Vegas ◊ Chicago ◊ Palm Beach

Published in the United States of America by
Histria Books
7181 N. Hualapai Way, Ste. 130-86
Las Vegas, NV 89166 USA
HistriaBooks.com

Histria Kids is an imprint of Histria Books. Titles published under the imprints of Histria Books are distributed worldwide.

Library of Congress Control Number: 2020938475

ISBN 978-1-59211-059-9 (casebound)
ISBN 978-1-59211-123-7 (softbound)
ISBN 978-1-59211-183-1 (eBook)

Contents

Introduction 9

Chapter One: Covering the Bases 11

Chapter Two: An Interesting Timeline 13

First Lady Moments: Jacqueline Kennedy 15

Chapter Three: The Young Republic, 1789-1829 16

First Lady Moments: Martha Washington 26

Chapter Four: The Frontier Years, 1829-1857 27

First Lady Moments: Dolley Madison 33

Chapter Five: A Changing Nation, 1857-1897 34

First Lady Moments: Nancy Reagan 48

Chapter Six: The Industrial Years, 1897-1921 49

First Lady Moments: Hillary Clinton 53

Chapter Seven: Prosperity And Failure, 1921-1945 54

First Ladies Moment: Grace Coolidge 57

Chapter Eight: Post-War, 1945-1969 58

First Ladies Moment: Eleanor Roosevelt 66

Chapter Nine: Crisis Years, 1969-1993 67

First Lady Moment: Rosalynn Carter 73

Chapter Ten: New Millenia, 1993-Present 74

First Lady Moment: Michelle Obama 85

Chapter Eleven Hail to the Chief 86

Presidents' Roll Call 88

Bibliography: 91

Answer Key (from pages 86-87) 93

This book is dedicated to all the teachers I had growing up who showed me that learning was fun, and to Disney's Imagineers whose imagination with robots and history in the Hall of Presidents attraction turned a little ten year old into a History nut.

Introduction

Have you ever been to Walt Disney World in Orlando? I can credit the Magic Kingdom for starting my fascination with presidential trivia. I'm sure it started back when I was a kid and went to Walt Disney World for the first time and discovered the Hall of Presidents. I sat in there with my family and watched the presidents come to life. I listened to Abraham Lincoln's speech and I was just in awe of the whole thing. Then, some time later, I happened across a fact book about the presidents that I used throughout my career as a student in public schools to brush up on presidential facts and for book reports. I will admit, not everyone is into all things presidential, but if you are holding this book in your hand then you have the same fascination with those who have held the top post in our great nation… or you needed something quick to help with a homework assignment. Either way, welcome to *Powerfully Perplexing Presidential Profiles*.

Rod Martinez

Chapter One: Covering the Bases

Ok, we have to cover the bases (basics). So, you know how you hear those fast quotes after car commercials and ad spots on the radio, where the guy is speaking so fast that you can't even understand what he's saying? Well this chapter is kind of like that, but I thought it was important to get this out first, and then we can jump into the fun! Plus, you can read it as fast (or slow) as you want.

It seems that every book I have ever read on the subject of presidential trivia or history always starts off with this one bit of trivia that by now everyone should know, but just in case you had the chicken pox that day your teacher filled everyone *else* in, these are the criteria, the rules. Ready?

To become the President of the United States you must:

- Be thirty-five years old or older.

- Be a natural born U.S. citizen

- Have lived in the United States at least 14 years straight.

- *You have to be filthy rich!*

Ok, I made up that last one, but in this day and age it seems that having gobs of green paper with president's faces on them is a qualifier, though it isn't. Andrew Johnson (you'll soon read about his story), who was probably our poorest President, made it to the White House and, hey, if he could do it, any of us could.

A lot of people have different ideas of what being President is. Back when our forefathers stood around a room in Philadelphia thinking this all out, they had different views too. Some thought he should be like a king, but many others – who were fighting England to get away from the king type of rule – wanted instead someone who would rule fairly, in a democratic government, where the people's say meant something. They finally agreed on an officer simply called – the President. But the office of President doesn't make him the ultimate ruler of the United States. The President has to share responsibilities with two other branches of government, the Congress and the Supreme Court. And each of those branches have some power over the other to make it a system of checks and balances. It's kind of like a game of *rocks, paper, scissors.*

So the President is like a CEO, the head of a company. The Congress is like the Board of Directors – the ones who make a lot of decisions – and the Supreme Court is like a committee to oversee that the other two are doing the right thing.

In this country, it's different than in others where you have to have privilege to gain power, or be in the family – like for example England, where the king or queen is always a member of the royal family. In the United States, we all have the freedom to strive to be President. When I was a little boy, I remember my dad telling me, "Son, you can be anything in this country, why you could even be President if you wanted!" Well I chose not to go that route, but now I'm telling you – *you can be President*, and if you're serious about that goal, you can make it, though it takes a lot of time and effort to make it to the Oval Office – which is the name of the office in the White House where the President works – and we're going to learn about some of the fun stuff that happened on the way to that office, or while occupying that office, or in some cases – trying to *leave* that office!

Chapter Two: An Interesting Timeline

Many people don't know this, but there's a direct line in history where a former President crossed paths with a future President – all the way from George Washington to Donald Trump – and by this I don't mean the next man that was in line, I mean someone who wasn't even remotely *thought* to be in line for future Presidency, and they just kind of crossed paths. If you don't believe me, read on and see for yourself...

- George Washington appointed *John Quincy Adams* (the son of Vice-President John Adams and later our 6th President) as minister to Holland.

- After his presidency, John Quincy Adams served in the House of Representatives. During a heated voting session, he suffered a stroke and among the witnesses there was a young man who was a Representative from Illinois. Though there is no record of them being friends, they definitely met and the young man was on the Committee of Arrangements for Adams' funeral along with several other Congressmen. That man's name was *Abraham Lincoln*.

- When Lincoln died, his funeral train procession passed through New York City by the home of a very prominent man in the Big Apple (another nickname for New York City). There is actually a photo of this event, if you look closely in the window you will see two figures, two little boys. One of them was the grandson of the man who owned the mansion, his name was *Theodore "Teddy" Roosevelt*, a future President.

- In 1905, President Teddy Roosevelt gave his niece away at her wedding. Her name was Eleanor Roosevelt, bride to *Franklin Delano Roosevelt* (who was her 5th cousin).

- During Franklin Roosevelt's presidency, he appointed a prominent Boston businessman as Ambassador to England. You may not remember him, but I'm sure you've heard of his son, *John F. Kennedy*.

- In 1963, the American Legion's *Boy Nation*, a civics group, was in Washington, D.C. and the group went to the White House to visit JFK. One of the boys there was a teenager from Arkansas who actually had his picture taken with Kennedy. Maybe you've heard of him? His name was *William Jefferson Clinton*, or Bill to his friends.

- In 2005, the Clintons were invited to a wedding of a wealthy New York businessman. Hillary Clinton attended the wedding and Bill later showed up for the festivities, they even took a couple of pictures with the new bride and groom, Melania and her new husband, Donald Trump who, 11 years later, became 45th President of the United States.

- On Dec. 19, 1972, the Apollo 17 space crew returned safely to Earth. Also, on this day, a phone call was placed from the White House to a young senator from Delaware. It wasn't business, it wasn't government. In fact, the man making the phone call wasn't really a big fan of the man he was calling, and that feeling went both ways. The man making the call was the Commander in Chief at the time, Richard Nixon. The man receiving the call was thirty-year-old Joe Biden, whose wife and one year old daughter were killed the day before in a car accident. The President was paying respect to the man who would almost forty years later take his spot as President of the United States.

- *????* Somewhere out there is a young man or woman who met Bill Clinton, or maybe George W. Bush, Barak Obama, or Donald Trump, and he or she will be next in line on this prestigious list, could it be you?

First Lady Moments:
Jacqueline Kennedy

Jacqueline Lee Bouvier was a child of privilege. She lived the good life, but then her parents divorced. That was hard for her to accept, but she learned to live through it. She traveled a lot, loved to take pictures, loved riding horses, and she learned French. She later met a young Senator from Massachusetts and they fell in love. Then, in September of 1953, they married and later had three children. One of them passed away as an infant. Jackie brought elegance to the White House and was diligent about bringing back the old furniture that used to sit in the Executive Mansion. She wanted to make certain that the White House was a place of beauty and class. Her worse day came on November 22, 1963 when she sat in the car beside her husband and saw him assassinated.

Chapter Three:
The Young Republic, 1789-1829

George Washington to John Quincy Adams

George Washington cut down a cherry tree when he was a little boy and his father approached him and asked "Son, do you know who cut down this tree?" He looked up at his father and said "I cannot tell a lie, father, I cut it down." Did this really happen? We were all told this story in school, but it was made up. It never really happened. Why would someone make up a story like that? Well, George Washington was a man of character. He was honest, he cared, and he was someone you could trust. His later biographers (people who write books about people's lives) wanted to make sure his character remained intact. Truthfully, George was a gentleman. As General of the Continental Army, he fought side by side with his men. At times, horses were shot from under him and he had bullet holes in his hat. In the cold of winter, he rallied the troops and gave them hope. Some believe we would have never won the war for independence had any other man *but* Washington been in charge.

Here's a question to think about it for a minute. Which President do you think has the most places named after him? Lincoln? Jefferson? Madison? Kennedy? Roosevelt? Well, that honor falls on George Washington, yes the "Father of Our Country" has over 120 cities and towns named after him and that doesn't even count schools, counties and even one state! I mean the State of Washington, not the State of Georgia! In case you're curious, Georgia was named after George II, who was king of England during colonial times.

Back when George Washington was President, the formal way to greet someone was to bow. It was a courteous way to say "Hello"; you'd approach the person and bow your head to them. John Adams followed this custom because it was how they had always done things before as British subjects. Thomas Jefferson (this guy certainly deserves credit for a lot of things) broke this tradition and started shaking hands. It stuck, and we're still doing it today.

George Washington had wooden teeth, right? Wrong. In his early twenties, he started losing his teeth. By the time he was President, George hardly had an original tooth in his mouth. The dentists of the day made him several dentures. They were made of many different things, including metal, hippopotamus ivory, elephant ivory, and horse teeth to name a few. But they were very uncomfortable. Think about it, ever seen a picture of him smiling?

Let's talk pants. Yes pants. You wear them, I wear them. It's been an American standard, well since America started, right? Nope. During the birth of our nation, women wore dresses and men wore knee breeches. What are knee breeches you ask? If you look at a full-length picture of George Washington, his 'pants' stop at his knees. Imagine the pants of a football player. That's the kind of 'pants' men wore back then. They actually wore stockings from the knee down under the breeches. So which President was first to wear trousers? It was James Madison, our fourth President. Before him, the guys were wearing the shorter man-version of Capri pants. For the record, John Quincy Adams was the first to wear them to his inauguration. Madison also developed the high-five slap. Ok, ok, I made that one up.

Do you know what a silent partner is? If you decided to start a club in school but you needed money to get stuff for it, like hats, or decals or jackets, you'd go to your Mom or Dad for it. They wouldn't really be members of the club, but they were your silent partners because they helped you get the stuff you needed. John Adams, our second President, felt like a silent partner. On his inauguration, as he was giving his speech, he could notice many of the people there staring at George Washington who sat behind him. Many of the people had tears in their eyes. George Washington was as loved in his day as he still is today. Though John Adams did a lot for the American fight for independence, he felt like a silent partner when he was around guys like Washington and Jefferson who were usually in the public eye.

If you go to Washington D.C. on vacation (I highly recommend it), you will step foot in one of the most historical cities in the United States. From one point in the mall, you can see the White House, Washington Monument, Lincoln Memorial, and Jefferson Memorial. Within walking distance are the Franklin Delano Roosevelt, Korean War, World War II, and even the Martin Luther King memorials. But there's another national monument that you will have to travel just a bit further to visit –all the way to the Black Hills of South Dakota. Mount Rushmore is a familiar sight to all of us, it's the mountain that has four Presidents' faces carved into it. Well, maybe not 100% 'carved' – unless you count dynamite as a carving tool. Here's a question, whose faces are on the mountain? If you guessed Washington, Jefferson, Lincoln, and Teddy Roosevelt then you would be right. But why did those Presidents get picked? Construction began in 1927 when Calvin "Silent Cal" Coolidge, our thirtieth president was in the White House. How did the sculptor pick these four out of the thirty he could choose from? He actually had a reason for the four he picked:

- **George Washington** was picked because of his role in the birth of the United States.

- **Thomas Jefferson** was picked for his authorship of the Declaration of Independence.

- **Abraham Lincoln** was picked because of his tireless fight to keep our nation together.

- **Theodore Roosevelt** was picked because of his contributions to business, and for bringing the United States into the 20th Century.

Do you like parties? My wife loves them! Do you know that there's a party that goes on full-time, non-stop? No, not the kind of party you're thinking of, though the word *party* does mean "a gathering of people," the party I'm talking about is a political party. Every President has been a member of a political party. You've probably heard of the two most popular ones – the Republican and Democratic parties, and maybe even the Tea Party because it's become popular. But there were many other parties out there that came and went. Abraham Lincoln was our first Republican President. The first Democratic President was Andrew Jackson. George Washington was a Federalist, there was even a Whig Party – no not because of their hair. Whig meant "against tyranny." Tyranny means having a king or ruler with absolute authority, who doesn't care about the people. The people who started the Whig Party thought that Jackson was a tyrant. There was even a Know Nothing Party that wanted to restrict immigration to the country, and a Bull Moose Party – started by Teddy Roosevelt when he tried to run for President a third term. Personally, I'm waiting for the Chocolate Milk Party!

When people get married, they sign a piece of paper stating that they will be together and stay together. When a person starts a business, he writes a business plan to let him and everyone else know what he plans to do with his business. When you start a club with friends, a lot of times you'll put together a form with rules of the club, like "No girls allowed" or "No boys allowed" or "No spinach beyond this point!" These are rules you run your club by. Back in the 1700s, the framers of the Constitution got together and started working on how they wanted to run this new country. They didn't want it to be like their old country, England. They wanted freedoms and guarantees of freedom. This paper made sure that everyone knew that they meant business. Two of the men who would later become Presidents signed the document, George Washington and James Madison. John Adams was away on diplomatic business at the time or he definitely would have signed it.

The United States capital wasn't always in Washington D.C. In fact, D.C. (which stands for District of Columbia) was an idea to place the capitol right smack in the middle of the country. Back in George Washington's day, the middle was, well exactly where it is now. The capitol was first in New York, and then moved to Philadelphia. Then, in 1800, it was moved from Philadelphia to Washington, D.C. Coincidentally, in January of that year, President Millard Fillmore was born.

Speaking of John Adams, even though he was the second President of the US, he had a couple of firsts. He was the first President to actually *live* in the White House. George Washington in the planning for the White House, but he never got to live in it. He was the only President who didn't. When John and his family moved in, it was still under construction. It was damp, dark, smelly and smoky. One of his sons who came to know the mansion as the home of his parents (he was 22 at the time), eventually came back to live there... as President. John Quincy Adams, John Adams' son, was elected President of the United States in 1825.

Here's another interesting story about two old friends, Tom and John – as in John Adams, our second President, and Thomas Jefferson, our third. These two men were also good friends who worked side by side to lay the foundation for this great country. They worked together on the Declaration of Independence, they talked a lot about the Constitution (though neither of them was at the Convention), they argued, laughed, and worked tirelessly to make sure that the United States would not turn into what England represented to them. Freedom was the most important thing that they fought for. Years later, they became bitter rivals and didn't speak to each other for ten years. But they finally set their differences aside because deep inside they knew that if not for their friendship and what they believed in and fought for, this country might not have ended up the way it did. They grew old and stayed in touch. Then one day – July 4th, 1826 - on the 50th anniversary of the signing of the Declaration of Independence, the document they held sacred and that they believed would make America the great country that it is today... they both died, just hours apart. Neither of them knew that the other was dying. John's last words were "Jefferson still survives."

You hear the term "American Revolution" all the time, do you know what it means? People came from England and established colonies here in the "New World" or "America" as it would be called later. Though they lived here, they still had to live by the rules of England. The King would pass laws and collect taxes. The colonists didn't like it so they decided to revolt – to start a revolution, which means "to fight against." They fought against the rules that the King of England had imposed on them. It came to a real bad spot one day in Boston when colonists started booing the red coat British soldiers. One thing lead to another and someone threw a stick and hit a soldier. The soldiers pulled out their rifles and started shooting. In the end, the first American to be killed was a man named Crispus Attucks. The soldiers got in trouble and were put on trial. They were defended by an American lawyer – though at the time he considered himself an "English subject." Of the eight soldiers tried in court, only two were convicted, and they both eventually got off. But the young lawyer thought he did a great job. He must have, he ended up years later becoming President of the United States, his name was John Adams.

Is there someone else in your class who has the same first name as you do? It's common, I had it happen in school when I was growing up. Then they had to come up with nicknames or call you by your first and last names to know who they were talking about. With all the Presidents we've had – which do you think is the most popular first name? I'll give you a hint, so far there have been six Presidents with this first name? What do you think it is, George? Fred? Steve? Ok, the number one *most popular* first name for U.S. Presidents is… drum roll please… *James*. There's James Madison, James Monroe, James K. Polk, James Buchanan, James A. Garfield and James (Jimmy) Carter. The second most popular is… well there's a tie: *John and William*, both with four Presidents each; John Adams, John Quincy Adams, John Tyler and John F. Kennedy – and then William Harrison, William McKinley, William Howard Taft and Bill (William) Clinton. Bill is the nickname for William. I guess you could say that the White House collected a lot of Bills, huh?

If you could pick one of these skills, which would you pick: to be a musician, writer, master gardener, architect, inventor, scientist or speaker of several languages? Well there was one man who occupied the White House who did all of these and more! Thomas Jefferson (my personal favorite President) did it all. Once in the 1960s, during a dinner in the Stateroom where John F. Kennedy had the best and brightest in the country seated with him, he said with a smile, "I think this is the most extraordinary collection of talent, of human knowledge, that has ever been gathered at the White House – with the possible exception of when Thomas Jefferson dined alone." Jefferson was a gentleman farmer who just happened to be full of talent and brains. Speaking of brains, in 1743, the year T.J. was born, Ben Franklin helped form the American Philosophical Society, which was like a club for scientists and smart men. It's ironic that later Jefferson would eventually join this club and work side by side with Franklin in framing this country.

What's a hot dog without ketchup? Hot dogs have been an American treat for ages, but could you imagine eating one without ketchup? Or even a burger, or fries without it? Well that could not have happened if it weren't for a red-head who ran the country years and years ago. Back in his day, tomatoes were thought to be poisonous. Though tomatoes were eaten and grown in other countries, many early Americans just weren't sure

about this fruit (it's not a vegetable). Some claim that Thomas Jefferson introduced tomatoes to the free world. That's really not 100% true, but he did grow them and he had no trouble eating them. Whether he brought them to the American table or not, he will forever be tied to them, so the next time you bite into a hot dog smothered in ketchup, smile and say, "Thanks Tom."

Some Presidents didn't really even *like* being President. You'll read about that later, but Thomas Jefferson did one even better. Before he died, he left instructions on what was to be written on his gravestone. On it, he listed everything he wanted to be noted for, and he didn't even mention being President! Here's what's written on his grave:

"Here was buried Thomas Jefferson, Author of the Declaration of American Independence, of the Statute of Virginia for Religious Freedom, Father of the University of Virginia."

Size really isn't an issue as far as the office of President of the United States is concerned. Our fourth President, James Madison, was five feet four inches tall, probably the height of many of your school mates. He only weighed about a hundred pounds, but the weight of this man on our government was huge. Mr. Madison is known as the *Father of Our Constitution* because he was instrumental along with our founding fathers in getting our Constitution to the point where we now know it. The Constitution is the document that is the backbone of the United States government. It's because of the Constitution that we run our country the way we do. It's a sacred document to many Americans, and most Congressmen carry a copy of it in the form of a booklet in their suit pockets every day. When the President is sworn in on January 20th every four years, he vows to "Preserve, protect and defend the Constitution", yes, it's *that* important. Until 1937, the President was inaugurated every four years on March 4.

July 4th is an important date to us Americans – Independence Day, the Fourth of July. It's filled with fireworks, Bar-B-Ques, and parades. You already read that two of our earliest Presidents died on July 4th in 1826. Well one more President died on July 4th, he was our fifth President, James Monroe. Monroe had a couple more distinctions; he's the only other President who won the vote unanimously. No one voted against George Washington. Monroe won all the electoral votes, except one, and they say it was because the man who voted against him only did it to keep George Washington as the only truly unanimous winner. Ever heard of a city called Monrovia? It's the capitol city of Liberia, a country in Africa. It's the *only* other capitol city named after a U.S. President besides our own Washington D.C. Oh, one more thing, we have one President who was actually *born* on July 4th, Calvin "Silent Cal" Coolidge.

First Lady Moments:
Martha Washington

    Martha Dandridge was born to a prominent Virginia family. She married a rich man, Daniel Custis, but he later died, leaving her and the kids with a 17,000 acre plantation. She was rich when she met Colonel George Washington and the two later married. They had no kids of their own. That's right – the Father of Our Country had no children, but he helped to raise Martha's kids with no problem.

Chapter Four:
The Frontier Years, 1829-1857

Andrew Jackson to Franklin Pierce

Andrew Jackson, our seventh President, was a very interesting man. It's not every day that an 'ordinary' man makes it to the White House. At least that's how he portrayed himself. Surely, Andrew Jackson, one of the most controversial men ever to hold the post of President, is so full of facts and information to fill a trivia book on its own. He was the only President who actually participated in a duel. A duel was a form of settling an argument back in those days; it's not something you would want to be a part of. How it worked was you and someone else had a disagreement and felt 'dishonored', so you'd meet in a field,

you'd both have a pistol in your hand, you stand back to back, take ten paces out, turn, and shoot. Whoever was still standing won the argument, silly huh? Andrew actually carried bullets in his body for years. Talk about tough. One day after walking out of a funeral, an ex-government employee approached him and took two gun shots at him. Jackson was hit, but he was so angry that he pulled out his cane and attacked his assailant. His body guards had to pull Jackson off the man because the President almost killed him. I'm not sure we've ever had a President as tough as him. I can hear Jackson now asking ... *"Who's Bad?"*

Are you an American Citizen? It's a question we take for granted now, but can you imagine if you went back in time and met our founding fathers and asked them that question? Truthfully, the first President who could boast that he was a true American Citizen, born in the United States, was our eighth President, Martin Van Buren. He was born in New York, *after* the Declaration of Independence was ratified. That means that after the Declaration was signed and we became the United Stated of America. Before that date in 1776, people in this country were still British subjects (or citizens of whatever country they came from). Old Kinderhook (Van Buren's nickname) could lay claim to being the first truly American President.

James K. Polk is forever linked to Tennessee. You ask any Tennessean and they will proudly boast his name as one of their premier statesmen from way back when, but he was born in North Carolina. That being said, Polk's presidency was duly noted for one particular event – during his term – music, parties, and dancing were not allowed in the White House. Because of their religious affiliation, his wife would not permit any rabble-rousing in the most important home in the United States.

At the beginning of this book, I pointed out the strange coincidences of Presidents meeting future Presidents of other generations. Well believe it or not, Abe Lincoln had *another* brush with a past President before he made it to the White House. In the summer of 1842, President Van Buren traveled to Illinois. They made a stop and among the people who were brought to meet him was a young lawyer – you guessed it, Lincoln. Van Buren later said that he laughed so hard at the jokes that Abe told him that his sides were still hurting. I think Lincoln would have been a great comedian today. By the way, 1842 was an important year in Lincoln's life; he almost fought in a duel with a man, plus it's the year he married his wife, Mary Todd. Wow, he was a busy man, huh?

Can you be President and be a doctor too? William Henry Harrison studied to be a doctor, but didn't finish. He would have been our only President M.D., but he ended up getting into politics. President Woodrow Wilson received a Ph.D. in college making him a doctor, but not a doctor of medicine. In college, a Ph.D. degree is the highest you can get and someone with a Ph.D. can be called a doctor. The D stands for doctorate. His degree was in political science.

I want you to think of something that you really don't like. Got it? Ok, if I gave you that item would you keep it? How about someone you don't like, could you forget your reason why you don't like them and decide to be friends with them, and maybe adopt them into your house and family? Well, Andrew Jackson didn't like Native-Americans (they called them Indians back then), I mean – he really didn't like them. He fought them in wars, he killed them, and he was even the main reason for the Trail of Tears, an event in American History that most people would rather forget, but that the Native Americans will never forget. Yet, Jackson did something that shocked even those closest to him. After a battle with the Red Stick Tribe where he and his army killed many, there was a little orphaned boy, his mother had been killed. Andrew Jackson took the kid and adopted him as his son.

Do you like your teacher? Do you *really* like your teacher? Well here's a first, our thirteenth President, Millard Fillmore, married his teacher. Of course, she was only two years older than him. His wife Abigail was the *first* First Lady that held a job before becoming First Lady. Man this is the *first* time I have used the word 'first' so many times. How many times is the word first in this paragraph? If you're the first to figure it out, you win *first prize*! Ok sorry, there's really no first prize.

Do you have a nickname? I bet it's one that your friends and family call you in a cute way, like Skippy, Franny, Junior, or Bubba, right? Well John Tyler, our tenth President, had a nickname too. They called him "*His Accidency*" because he became President *by accident*. The accident they were talking about was the sudden death of President Harrison who died from pneumonia just a month after being inaugurated as President. So they said Tyler, his Vice-President, "accidentally" became President. He wasn't too fond of the nickname. He had another interesting distinction; John Tyler served as President of the United States, but sometime after he left office, his home state of Virginia decided to *secede* from the Union (that means, they broke away from the Unites States) to form the Confederate States of America. At first, he opposed the idea, but when his State went through with it, he joined the Confederate Congress. Tyler became the only U.S. President to serve under the Confederacy too.

How would you like to be the *daughter* of a President and the *wife* of a President? So far, only one woman can hold claim to that. Her name was Sarah Knox Taylor. She was the daughter of President Zachary Taylor, but he wasn't President just yet. She married Jefferson Davis, who would eventually become President of the Confederate States. She died at age 21, years before either man became President, but she still holds the claim. Her father also served as an officer in the Black Hawk War – which incidentally Abraham Lincoln served in, though he saw no combat.

CSI is a popular show on TV. They have police officers that are scientists and they follow clues after someone dies. They figure out the cause of death or who did it. We're used to that these days, but they sure could have used a CSI team back in the mid 1800s. When President Zachary Taylor died after only sixteen months in office, it was a mystery. Ok, put on your detective hats, we need to solve this: Fact 1 – it was July 4th and those living in Washington D.C. were celebrating the building of the Washington Monument. Fact 2 – The President was there with everyone else and seemed to enjoy himself, in fact on this hot day he enjoyed an interesting snack of a bowl of cherries and an ice cold glass of milk. Fact 3 – a few days later he started complaining about cramps. Fact 4 – Five days later, he died. Medical science was pretty primitive back then compared to what it is now, was he poisoned? Did someone feed him a bad cherry? Was the milk spoiled? Was it Voldemort? It still remains a mystery, though they believe it was a mixture of bacteria, bad milk or… something else.

Can you imagine going to take a bath and turning on the faucet and no water comes out? How about going to the kitchen to turn on the stove and… there's no stove? We take these things for granted now, but President Millard Fillmore was the first President to have a bathtub with running water. Before that they just had a tub they filled with water from buckets – and honestly – people didn't bathe as often as we do now. He was also the first President to have a stove in the White House, before the stove they just had an open pit they'd light a fire in. I wonder if he had a Twitter account?

You would think that living in the White House is a wonderful thing and it *has* been for many families that called it home, but when President Franklin Pierce and his wife moved in, back in 1853, their beloved son Bennie had just died in a tragic train accident earlier that year. He was only eleven years old and Franklin's wife was sad the whole time he was President. Honestly, neither of them ever got over it, and though Pierce was known as a handsome President, his sadness followed him everywhere. Of the three sons he had, none of them saw him make it to the Presidency.

Which President do you think had the most kids? Buchanan had none, Washington had none of his own, Bill Clinton had just one daughter – think about it. If you had lots of kids, you must really like kids. President Tyler had fifteen kids! Ok well, his wives did anyway (he was married twice). But John Tyler really liked kids. He said that he loved to have babies around, in fact, guess what he was doing when he found out that he'd become President? He was playing marbles with his sons. Tyler had so many children that as of 2018 two of his grandsons were still living!

First Lady Moments:
Dolley Madison

Dolley Payne was born in North Carolina. Her first husband died of yellow fever and she met James Madison. Even though Jefferson was President at the time, Dolley helped with most of the social functions at the White House, so by the time her husband became President, everyone knew her. Dolley is most famous for saving the painting of George Washington when the British burned down the White House during the War of 1812, she refused to leave the mansion until several important papers and the painting were saved.

Chapter Five:
A Changing Nation, 1857-1897

James Buchanan to Grover Cleveland

Every President had a First Lady, right? Well. kind of. There was only one President who didn't have a wife, James Buchanan. He was once engaged to someone, but they broke up and later she passed away. He was so heart-broken that he promised he'd never marry – and he didn't. So when he later became President... there was no First Lady! His niece filled the role for him though, and she did a pretty good job. Buchanan was the President before Lincoln, after he left office in 1861, he lived only seven more years and died in June of 1868. Incidentally, the first traffic lights were installed later that year. Not in the United States, but in England. Did they even have cars yet?

At least half of our Presidents served in the military in one way or another. Some had major roles, some had minor ones, or even civilian (meaning they didn't actually join, but they served as citizens) roles. In the Army, being a General is the top job you can have. George Washington was a General, so were Grant, Harrison, Eisenhower, and *Arthur* to name a few. Chester A. Arthur was an interesting man. You usually think of military types as rough and tough, but Chester was pretty elegant. He was considered a gentleman in his day. He was known to change his pants more than once a day just for fashion's sake. He was even approached by some women who asked *him* to marry *them*. An interesting thing about his presidency is that he didn't have a Vice-President. He became President because the one before him died and they just never got around to getting a Vice. Plus, he didn't deliver an Inaugural Address. The address isn't the number on the White

House (which is 1600 Pennsylvania Avenue, Washington D.C., by the way), it's the speech a new President gives when he's sworn in to office.

June 1st isn't a date important to a lot of people, unless it happens to be your birthday. But in American history, several things happened on this date in different years; In 1869 – inventor Thomas A. Edison patented the first voting machine. In 1880, the first pay telephone was installed (unfortunately, we don't use those anymore – everyone has a cell phone now). In 1868, President James Buchanan died. If you are a fan of old movies, the famous American actress Marilyn Monroe was born in 1926.

Do you have a middle name? If you put together the first letters of your first, middle and last name do they spell anything? Well, rumor has it that one of our Presidents changed his name because of his initials! He was born *Hiram Ulysses Grant* and when he entered West Point, one of the most prestigious military schools in the country, the rumor is that he didn't want to be known as HUG, so he changed his name to Ulysses S. Grant. Good thing his name wasn't **Hiram Angus Mikowitz**! Of course, the truth is that his name was entered as Ulysses Simpson (Simpson was his mother's maiden name) Grant by mistake and he just went with it.

Speaking of Grant, he was probably the only President to get a speeding ticket while President. And not in a car, mind you, remember they didn't have cars back then. The President was stopped by a Washington DC cop for speeding with his horse and buggy! At first, when the officer realized who he was, he backed off and didn't want to give him the ticket, but Grant insisted and commended him for doing his job. If only he had Henry Ford (founder of Ford Motor Company) around, he could have slapped a speedometer on that buggy, but then again, Henry was a little kid at the time.

Do you know what "suffrage" is? No, it isn't you having to eat the spinach your mom cooked last night, suffrage means the *right to vote*. In the beginning of our government, believe it or not, women weren't allowed to vote. They took their cause to the streets. They were angry, after all they were Americans too, right? Many history books and classrooms tell you that in the early 1900s and especially the 1920s, the Women's Suffrage Movement finally came to light and the country took note, but back in 1890, President Benjamin Harrison hired the very first woman staffer in the White House. It was a big push for the movement, but you've probably never heard of her, she's rarely ever mentioned in history class (I don't know why, I think we should all know her name). Her name was Alice Sanger.

Being President of the United States would be the top post that anyone would want to strive to get, right? After all, you're the "leader of the free world," as they say. So if you were elected President and served maybe two full terms (eight years) what else would you do after you left office? Would you look for another job in government? Believe it or not, many ex-presidents did, but to date only a few have done it. William Howard Taft went on to become a Chief Justice of the Supreme Court, John Quincy Adams served in the House of Representatives (and died there), John Tyler also served in the House of Representatives – but for the "other side" – the Confederacy, and Andrew Johnson became a Senator.

The year 1881 was an interesting one in American politics. We had three Presidents in one year! Rutherford B. Hayes was the outgoing President and handed the torch to James Garfield. Garfield has the distinct honor of being the second President to be assassinated while in office. He served only 200 days, so his Vice-President took over the role of President. All of this happened in one year. Coincidentally, forty years before, Martin Van Buren stepped down and new President William Henry Harrison took over, he died a month after being in office (from pneumonia), and his Vice-President, John Tyler took over. I guess now when your mom says "cover up, you don't want to catch pneumonia," you'll listen, huh?

When you think of war heroes that ended up making it into the office of the President, you think of Grant, Washington, and Eisenhower, but how about Hayes? Rutherford B. Hayes fought in the Civil War as an officer, but also he has a distinction among those who eventually made it to the oval office. Rutherford was the only of those back in that time that was actually wounded in the war. He almost lost his arm after one battle, but the doctors managed to save it. He was willing to have his arm cut off, but they knew they could save it. He also had four horses shot from under him.

Have you ever thought about writing your life story? Most people have very interesting things they could tell. Of course, you have all of your life to write a memoir, but people usually wait until they're older. Most Presidents write a memoir after they leave office and it's usually a best seller. But Ulysses Grant waited a bit longer. In fact, when he was diagnosed with throat cancer, he realized he didn't have a lot of money in the bank to leave his wife and kids, so he decided to hurry up and write his memoir. *Personal Memoirs* by Ulysses S. Grant was completed just three days before he died!

Johnny was an actor. He was a pretty famous actor, and everyone knew him. In fact, back in his day in the 60's he was one of the most loved and respected actors in the country. Whenever he starred in a show, people would come from miles around to see him. One April night, he went to the theater. He didn't go to perform, or to meet his fans. He didn't even go to rehearse. He had something else in mind. Johnny was mad, he was upset because he didn't like where the country was going, he didn't like the politics, he didn't like the direction, and he didn't like the President. So he decided to do something about it. He got some friends together and they planned to kill the leader of the United States! And he knew the President was going to be at the theater that night. As the audience enjoyed themselves, he snuck upstairs to where the President and his wife were sitting in their private booth, and he opened the door, pulled out a small gun, and in a split second, he took down the leader of the free world. That President was the first ever to be assassinated. It was in 1865, and he was Abraham Lincoln. Johnny – or John Wilkes Booth as his adoring fans knew him - had killed the President of the United States.

Secrets are a part of the job. The President has a lot of things he has to keep to himself; national secrets, passwords, staff issues, and… surgery? Well believe it or not, President Grover Cleveland had surgery and no one but the people closest to him knew about it. Doctor's found cancer in his mouth and had to remove some of his jaw. To keep it secret, they went on a boat and made it look like the President was just hanging out with friends, but he was really having surgery – on the boat! They replaced the removed jaw with a new one and no one knew about it until after Cleveland died! So be honest, how long would it take 'til your friends found out on Facebook that you just got a tooth pulled?

Andrew Johnson was Vice-President under Lincoln and became President after his assassination. Johnson grew up poor. Truthfully, he was probably the poorest of the men to hold the top office of Commander-in-Chief (another phrase for President). He was so poor that he became an indentured servant (so was the

13th President, Millard Fillmore), meaning he would intern with someone to learn a trade in return for being the person's servant for a certain period of time. That was something common back in those days. He became the intern of a tailor. A tailor is someone who makes clothes. In due time, Andrew grew up and became very good at tailoring, so needless to say he was probably one of the White House's snappiest dressers.

Can you imagine living in a house with no telephone? Eighteen Presidents did just that. It wasn't until Rutherford B. Hayes was in the White House when a telephone got installed, and he was three Presidents after Lincoln! They did, however have telegraphs and Morse Code and all that. The White House grew with the times and the country. Speaking of President Hayes, his wife and he didn't drink alcohol, and they wouldn't permit it to be served in the White House so she was famously called "Lemonade Lucy" because she would serve anything *but* alcohol while her husband was President. "Lemonade Lucy" by the way, was the first woman to hold the title "First Lady" (which is the title of the wife of the President), before then – there was no official title.

Lemonade
5 Cents

Who do you think was the best President of all time? *That* is not a trick question, it's a matter of opinion. If you ask most historians, they will say that Lincoln was. Not so much because of who he was, but because of the circumstances… the timing, and how he handled it. When Abraham Lincoln was President, our country split in two. It was the North against the South. People from each side of the country had their own opinions on how they thought this country should be run, and the Southern states seceded from the United States (remember what that means? There will be a test). Many historians wonder what would have happened to the country if say, Thomas Jefferson was President during this time, or George Bush, or Lyndon Johnson, or Barak Obama. Would we still have ended up the country we are today, united under one flag? Lincoln was determined in his decisions during the Civil War. Many think it was because of his humble nature, and the fact that he cherished this nation and didn't want us to divide, that his leadership kept us as one. But he was killed for his devotion to this country, and that is why he remains in the hearts of Americans to this day.

Ready to play detective again? This is a tough one. Mary and John got married, had some kids. They had a nice big roomy home in the hills near the nation's capital. John later died and left Mary with the kids and she struggled to make it. She decided to turn her house into a boarding house – a place where strangers and travelers could come and rent a room to rest. That worked for her and she had business. Then some young men started having meetings there at her place. They had plans to do something, something bad. One of the men's names was John Wilkes Booth (sound familiar?). Finally, the men – including one of her sons – set out to do their bad deed, to kill President Lincoln. After Booth died (just a few days after Lincoln did), the country wanted answers. Who did this, did John Wilkes Booth do it alone? Did he have people who worked with him? The police went to Mary's house, they arrested her, they took her to trial, and then took her to prison. Mary Surratt became the first woman executed (killed) in the United States because they thought she had something to do with Lincoln's death. What do you think?

Has anyone ever called you "two-faced"? If they did, don't smile, it wasn't a compliment. Being called 'two-faced' means you'll say one thing to make one person happy, then another thing to make another person happy. Like, say someone asked you what your favorite color was and you know it's red. You say red because your best friend likes red too, but you know that your other best friend likes green. So you tell one person it's red, but you tell the other person it's green, that's being 'two-faced.' Abraham Lincoln was called two-faced once and being as he never considered himself a handsome man, he replied, "If I had two faces, do you think I'd be wearing this one?"

Lincoln was clearly one of our funniest Presidents. He loved to joke and one of his favorites was telling puns. Puns are a way of playing with words, you can say one thing, but mean another thing. He was walking with the Secretary of State one time and passed by a shop where the business owner's name was on the window. Lincoln read it out loud. "T.R. Strong," then he smiled, "...coffee are strong, too." Get it? "T", as in tea – the drink? The Secretary cracked a smile, but he didn't laugh. Would *you* have laughed?

You'd think that winning an election and becoming President of the United States was a good thing. With so many other candidates running against you, the odds of making it have to be big. So you'd consider yourself lucky if you won, right? Of all the Presidents, Abraham Lincoln could probably tell you that it was a long road to getting to 1600 Pennsylvania Avenue. Before he became President, he had a list of failures that would have probably discouraged any other man. He ran for the Illinois legislature, lost. When his business failed, he spent years paying what he owed. He fell in love with someone, they got engaged – and she died. He ran for Congress, and lost. Ran for Senate – lost. Ran for Vice-President – lost. Two of his sons passed away. But he didn't quit, and thanks to his 'never give up' attitude, he became one of the greatest Presidents this country has ever had.

Have you ever invented anything? Inventions are cool, you come up with an idea that no one else has and if you get a patent on it – which is a registration in your name saying that you invented it, then no one can steal it form you. You make money with your invention by getting a patent. Well I told you earlier that Thomas Jefferson was an inventor, but he wasn't the only one (he didn't patent his inventions either). Can you guess who the other President is who invented something? Believe it or not, it was Abraham Lincoln. He invented a hydraulic device that could lift ships over shoals, the thing was never manufactured though. Do you have an idea for something? Maybe you should get to work on drawing plans for it, after you finish reading this book, I mean.

Ever have a bad dream that you couldn't stop thinking of after you woke up? Abraham Lincoln was troubled by a nightmare he had days before his assassination. He finally opened up and shared it with a friend. He told him that in the dream he had woken up in his bedroom when he heard a lot of sobbing and cries. He walked out to the hallway and down to the East Room and saw a casket. There were soldiers surrounding it and voices of mourners. He walked up to a soldier and asked who had died. He was told "The President, he was assassinated." He soon after woke up.

There is one other man, who was president but did not get to live in the White House, can you guess who he was? This is definitely a trick question. The trick is the word President, I didn't say "U.S. President." Of course you can answer that now with "The President of Microsoft" or "The President of Toyota!" so before this gets out of hand, the man's name was Jefferson Davis. Ever heard of him? He lived in a White House, but it wasn't in Washington DC, it was in Richmond, Virginia. Mr. Davis was President of the Confederate States of America. Yes, during the Civil War, the South had its own White House and its own President. He served the Confederacy, while Lincoln served for the Union.

Are you right handed or left handed? Can you write your name with your other hand and have it look legible, like you wrote it with your 'good' hand? It's hard to do, isn't it? Can you imagine being able to write your name with either hand and it would look like either hand was your 'good' hand? Ok how about

writing a sentence like "I like hotdogs, with ketchup," with both hands? That would be really hard, especially if I asked you to do it at the same time with both hands, right? Ok well suppose someone could write whole sentences with both hands, at the same time, in two different languages? Impossible, you say? Well, we had a President that could do that. President James Garfield could write with both hands, at the same time, one in Latin and one in Greek.

What's your favorite candy bar? Snickers? Mars? Almond Joy? There's a candy bar that is closely tied to a President. Back in 1921, when this candy bar was introduced, there was a very popular baseball player named Babe Ruth. Naturally everyone assumed that the Baby Ruth bar was named after him. There is still a lot of controversy over this, but the company itself claimed that the delicacy was named for Grover Cleveland's first daughter, Ruth Cleveland, though she was long dead after the candy bar came out. Still, some people believe that it was named after the baseball legend, but I guess we'll never know for sure.

These days, a President can only have two consecutive terms. That means he can serve his four years and if he gets elected again, he can serve another four years, but he cannot run again. We all know that Franklin Roosevelt had the longest term as President. He served from 1932, when he was first voted into office, all the way to the beginning of his fourth – yes *fourth* term. He died in 1945 during his fourth term. Soon after that, they made a rule whereby no man could serve more than two terms. But there was another President who served two terms, but they weren't consecutive, that is, back to back. Stephen *Grover* Cleveland (he didn't like to use his first name) became the 24th President in the mid 1880s. After the end of his first term, Benjamin Harrison won the role, but four years later, Grover Cleveland moved *back* into the White House after winning his second term! Benjamin Harrison, coincidentally, was the grandson of former President William Henry Harrison, the only grandson of a President to make it to the top office!

Grover Cleveland has another interesting fact. No, Cleveland, Ohio wasn't named after him (it was named after Moses *Cleaveland* – that's not a mistype – who was a surveyor and lawyer). Grover was the only (so far) President to get married in the White House, and he married the youngest First Lady ever, she was twenty-one. First Lady is the title given to the wife of the President – which makes you wonder. If a woman gets elected President, what would we call her husband… First Dude?

You wake up in the middle of the night, in your room. It's dark. You want to go to the kitchen and get a glass of water, how will you know where you're going in the dark? Well that's simple, flip the light switch on, right? Can you imagine not having that switch there, or worse, not wanting to flip that switch because – *gulp* – you're afraid to? They make fun of kids who are afraid of the dark, but we had a President who was scared to turn on the light! President Benjamin Harrison had his reasons, electricity was first installed in the White House during his Presidency and he just didn't trust electricity, he was scared of it. So he would have the staff turn the lights on and off for him. Coincidentally, he was the first President to have the White House Christmas tree put in the White House. I wonder what he did for Christmas lights?

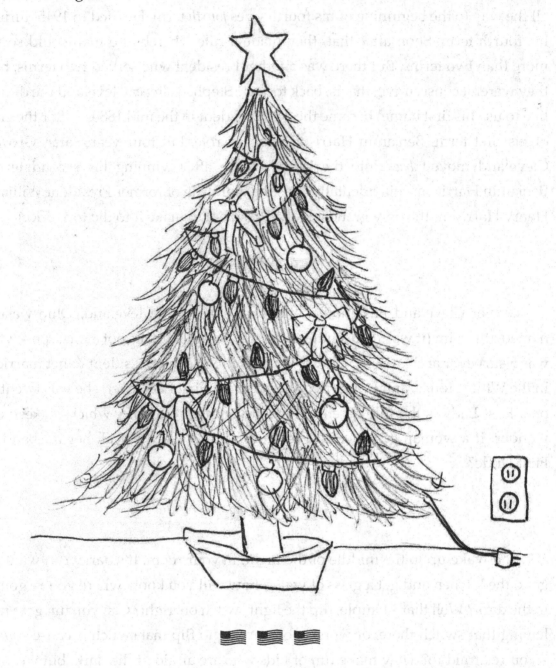

Tecumseh was a mighty warrior for his people, the Shawnee tribe. He opposed the United States and with good reason, this land was his before it was ours. Some say it was a curse, some say it was coincidence, but every President since William Henry Harrison (who he fought against in war) and John F. Kennedy who has been elected in a year that ended with a zero has been assassinated or died *while in office*. This is called Tecumseh's Curse. Four died by assassination: Lincoln,

Garfield, McKinley and Kennedy, and three died from other causes: Harrison, Harding and Franklin Roosevelt. Then in 1980, Reagan was elected. There was an assassination attempt on him, but he survived. George Bush was elected into office in 2000 and he lived through both of his terms, so some consider Reagan to have broken the 'curse'.

First Lady Moments:
Nancy Reagan

    Anne Frances Robbins was born in 1921. Sometime during her childhood, she got the nickname "Nancy". Her father was a salesman and her mother was an actress and they divorced. She was raised by her aunt and uncle in Maryland. Nancy later grew a love for acting and it was through acting that she met her husband, Ronald Reagan. Once they married, she gave up acting to become mother and wife. Nancy was known throughout her husband's Presidency for her campaign against drugs. Ever heard the phrase "Just Say No to drugs"? That was her campaign and she really worked hard to help young people stay away from drugs.

Chapter Six:
The Industrial Years, 1897–1921

William McKinley to Woodrow Wilson

Do you have an annoying little brother or sister? Don't worry, you're not alone, seems they're everywhere, in fact even in the White House. Teddy Roosevelt was having an important meeting one day and his little daughter Alice kept popping in and out of the room. Finally the man asked, "Theodore isn't there anything you can do to control Alice?" The President smiled and answered, "I can do one of two things, I can control Alice or I can be President, but I cannot possibly do both!"

Do you have a teddy bear? If you do or did, you can thank Theodore "Teddy" Roosevelt for it. Teddy was a sportsman who liked to hunt. On one of his expeditions, he was looking for bears and he had no luck. Later some guides found a bear and showed it to Teddy. He looked at it, then refused to shoot. When the story got out, a cartoonist drew a picture of the scene, everybody saw it, and a toy company jumped into the production of "Teddy" bears. They have been a hit ever since.

Teddy Roosevelt was known as one of the roughest, toughest men who ever occupied the White House. He was a member of the Rough Riders (which was a volunteer unit of the Army back in the late 1800s), he liked to box, he took care of his body, he was an outdoorsman who liked hunting, fishing, fought in a war, all that stuff. But would you believe that when he was young, Teddy Roosevelt was a thin child who was sick a lot? It's true. Teddy's Dad told him that he'd have to buff himself up to get better and to defend himself from bullies. That's funny when you realize that Teddy was the President who's famous line was "Speak softly, but carry a big stick" and his even more famous bark of *Bully!* when he really liked something.

Why is the White House called **The White House**? Well *duh*, it's painted white for one. But was it always called the White House? Truthfully, the answer is "no." It wasn't until Teddy Roosevelt was in office that the name *officially* became The White House. Before then, it was called The Executive Mansion, or the President's Palace, or even the President's house. Rumor says that it was painted white to hide the burn marks after the British set fire to it during the War of 1812. That's one of those stories that sounds true so it just has to be, but in reality, it started getting an overcoat of white to protect its sandstone construction from the elements. Obviously it works, the building is still standing today. So next time you build a sandcastle, cover it with a coat of paint so your great-great-great-great grandkids can enjoy it. Ok I'm kidding, don't do that. No one wants a mess of white paint on the beach!

I want to tell you about Major Archibald "Archie" Butt. No, he wasn't a President, Archie was a military man. He was a single man who never married and became an aide to President Teddy Roosevelt and later William Howard Taft. Both Presidents considered him a vital part of their staff. He was the man you leaned on to get things done and he never complained. Archie agreed to take a trip to Europe on business and would later return on another ship. President Taft had no worries that Archie would be back home soon and tending to the job that it seemed no one could do better than him. The Major got on the ship, but he never came back. The date was April 14th, the year was 1912. To most historians, it's a date they will never forget – the day the Titanic sank. Many lives were lost and each person on that vessel had a life story. Archie was one of the men who made sure that the women and children were put safely on their life boats and set out to the cold freezing waters. The President broke out in tears when he heard the news. In fact, it was a day of mourning for a lot of people in Washington D.C., Archie was a very loved man.

William Taft was the biggest President. I don't mean in popularity. Mr. Taft weighed over 300 pounds when he occupied the White House. Not that weight matters when it comes to holding the job, but they had to make a special bath tub for him. Big Bill (that was his  nickname) is buried at Arlington National Cemetery – the same place where John F. Kennedy was laid to rest. He was the only President to also hold the job of Chief Justice of the Supreme Court (judge), and he was prouder of *that* than being a President.

Tommy was born in Virginia, but soon afterwards, his family moved to Georgia. His dad was a minister so Tommy lived a pretty straight life. He witnessed a couple of things in his first ten years of life that would inevitably change his course; he just didn't know it at the time. At age four, one of his first memories was of listening to man walk by the front gate of his house and mention the fact that Abraham Lincoln had just won the election and that the country would most probably go to war. Not too long after that, living in Georgia, he remembered seeing several scenes from the Civil War (Or the "War Between The States" as the Southerners called it), including Union soldiers marching through town, his mother tending to wounded Confederate soldiers and even General Robert E. Lee with Union soldiers after his surrender. Tommy's family eventually moved to several other states and he grew up to become an incredible scholar. Tommy didn't like his first name – Thomas – so he dropped it and forever went by his middle and last names, which are more familiar to us, his name was Woodrow Wilson.

So, how much money does a President make? After all, it's a job, right? Well like most jobs in America, the salary has changed throughout the years. When George Washington was elected, he made $25,000 a year. Then in 1873 it went up to $50,000, in 1909 it went up to $75,000, then in 1949, $100,000. When Nixon was elected in 1969 it doubled to $200,000, then finally in 2001, it doubled again to $400,000. So maybe when you get into office you can just make it a cool million?

As you just read, William Howard Taft made it to the Supreme Court after he left the White House, when President Warren G. Harding appointed him as Chief Justice, but that didn't keep him away from the Presidency. The Chief Justice has the role of administering the oath of office to the President, so Mr. Taft had the privilege of swearing in two Presidents, Calvin Coolidge and Herbert Hoover. I guess he could have given them some good advice about living in the White House, don't you think?

First Lady Moments:
Hillary Clinton

    Hillary Diane Rodham was born in 1947. In the 60s she heard a speech given by Martin Luther King, Jr. and it inspired her to work in public service. She met her husband Bill Clinton in college. Little did she realize how much her life would circle American Politics, she studied to be a lawyer. Hillary became First Lady when Bill was elected, but after he left office she became a Senator. Then, when Barak Obama became President, he asked her to be his Secretary of State. She also ran an unsuccessful campaign for President. Many people thought she'd make a great President.

Chapter Seven:
Prosperity And Failure, 1921-1945

Warren G. Harding to Franklin D. Roosevelt

When you need something to start cooking in the kitchen, you usually have to go to the kitchen cabinet. The cabinet has everything you need to get the job done. The President has a cabinet too, but his Cabinet is the staff surrounding him and who help advise him. The Cabinet has grown big time since the days of George Washington. It is supposed to be hand-picked by the President from people who have the knowledge, skill and determination to get the job done. The posts they have include their own staff, and lots of taxpayer money to pay for staff and equipment and all the rest that goes with it. The worst thing a President could do is assign these jobs to old buddies and pals or people who have no idea how to get the job done. He'd pick them for other reasons like he thinks they're cool, or maybe they gave his campaign money to help him win. Common sense would tell you that something like that wouldn't happen, but it does and did. Warren Harding paid for it a hard way. Harding was elected President in 1920. He was a popular President and well-liked, but he gave jobs to people who took advantage of their posts. It marked his presidency and made him, even to this, day one of the Presidents most historians pick in the top 10 of bad ones. That isn't really fair when he accomplished some things that Presidents even today are trying to do without much luck, like fix money problems.

When a President is sworn in at his Inauguration (the day he officially takes over as President), it's a big deal and is usually held at the Capitol Building in Washington DC, but there were two instances where Washington DC wasn't even close to where the President was sworn in. Back in 1963, when President Kennedy was shot, they hustled Vice-President Johnson back to Air Force One. Judge Sarah Hughes swore him in, standing right between his wife and the wife of JFK. It was the first and only time in history – so far – that a President was sworn in on a plane and done so by a woman. Earlier in the 1920s, after President Harding's death, Vice President Calvin Coolidge was sworn in by his father, who was a Justice of the Peace (kind of like a judge), in Vermont. It was the first and only time so far that a father had sworn in his son as President.

Suppose someone came up to you at a party and said "I made a bet with someone that I can make you say more than two words." How would you answer them? You'd probably say "No you won't." Well guess what? They just made you say more than two words.

Someone approached our 26th President Calvin Coolidge like that at a party. He was rumored to be someone who didn't like to talk a lot – don't you wish you had friends like that? Anyway, he replied "You Lose."

Did you ever wish that you knew another language so you could talk to your friends and other people around you wouldn't know what you were saying? Some people use Pig-Latin for that, but so many people know Pig-Latin now that it just doesn't work anymore. In his earlier years, Herbert Hoover and his wife lived in China for two years. They both picked up on the language and would use it in later years to talk to each other when they didn't want people to know what they were saying. When he finally made it to the White House as our 31st President, he was the first to actually have a phone on his desk in the Oval Office. I wonder if he ordered Chinese on it?

Think you couldn't possibly have anything in common with a President? Barak Obama collects comic books. Franklin Roosevelt collected stamps. Rutherford Hayes played chess. Richard Nixon and Harry S Truman played piano. Many Presidents played golf. Lincoln and Kennedy loved to read. Dwight Eisenhower loved to paint, and John Quincy Adams collected coins.

Ok, so we've learned a lot about our Presidents, some were in the military, many went to college, some were athletes, a tailor, lawyers, businessmen. How about – a cheerleader? If I were to ask you how many Presidents you think were cheerleaders, what would be your answer? One? Two? Three? Well try four. Yes four of our Commanders-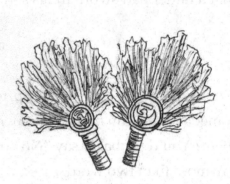in-Chief really were cheerleaders in college. Really? Really. In the early days of cheerleading, believe it or not, it was an all-male sport. Girls got in later, but four of the top dogs busted out the cheers. George W. Bush for Phillips Academy in Massachusetts, Ronald Reagan for Eureka College in Illinois, Dwight D. Eisenhower at West Point Academy, and Franklin D. Roosevelt at Harvard. So join me in a cheer… "Hail to the Chief sis-boom-ba! Hail to the Chief, Ra-ra-ra!"

Are you superstitious? Some people are, you know, they won't walk under a ladder, they're afraid of black cats, they think a broken mirror is bad luck? Well we had a President who was really superstitious. Franklin Delano Roosevelt was afraid of the number 13. If he had a meeting and there were 13 people, he'd invite someone else to join. He wouldn't have meetings on the 13th, wouldn't travel on the 13th. I wonder if – when he was little – he just skipped from age 12 to 14?

First Ladies Moment:
Grace Coolidge

Grace Anna Goodhue graduated from the University of Vermont in 1902 to become a teacher. She wanted to work with deaf children, teaching them to communicate by lip reading, rather than by signing. In 1904, she met and fell in love with Calvin Coolidge and the two were married the next year. When Calvin became President, Grace worked to support charitable organizations like the Red Cross. After her husband died in 1933, she continued to work with deaf children and during World War II she even worked to help Jewish refugees from Europe fleeing the Holocaust.

Chapter Eight:
Post-War, 1945-1969

Harry S Truman to Lyndon Johnson

Let's go back to nicknames for a second. Some of us had some really interesting ones growing up. Sometimes you get a nickname from a family member, sometimes from friends at school, or a teacher or people you work with. The President has a nickname too, no not from his wife or Mom, they have official nicknames that the Secret Service call them. Here's a list of some: John F Kennedy – Lancer, George W. Bush – Trailblazer, Richard Nixon – Searchlight, Ronald Reagan – Rawhide, Barak Obama – Renegade, Dwight David Eisenhower – Providence, Harry Truman – General, Gerald Ford –Pass Key, Jimmy Carter – Deacon, and Bill Clinton – Eagle. Some of the names have something to do with their character or some other thing about them. So, when you become President, what's the Secret Service going to call you?

The White House is a pretty old building. Think about it, if you were to ask someone in your town where the oldest building was, it might be 100 years old, or 75 years old. The White House is over two hundred years old! That's older than your math teacher! It's been through a lot. Back during the War of 1812, the British troops torched it and it was burned. Then later in the late 1940s, President Truman noticed a sagging floor and other issues within the building and had men look at it. They told him that the building was falling apart and would have to be redone from the ground up, how sad! Our White House needed a facelift. Well they decided to keep the outside intact. They didn't touch it, but they totally destroyed the inside and made it new again – new floors, new walls, new ceilings, I think they even shampooed the dog! Other Presidents have added or taken away from the White House, a bowling alley here, a small theater there. One President had an indoor pool put in, then another President had them fill it with cement and turn it into a room!

Do you have a middle name? Many Americans do, but it isn't really important to have one. Well to some people anyway, we have a President whose middle name caused so much controversy in his family that he *has* a middle name, yet he *doesn't*. When Harry Truman was born, there was a discussion about what his middle name should be. Both his parents wanted to name him after their fathers, Shippe or Solomon, but they couldn't agree – so they compromised. They named him Harry S Truman. The S doesn't stand for anything, S is his middle name. I wonder if they asked the midwife for her opinion on this one?

Many Presidential elections are close until the end. Back in 1948, it was one for the books. Harry Truman was running against Thomas Dewey. It was a close race, but all bets were on Dewey. That night, Truman went to bed knowing he had lost. Then he woke up the next day to find that he had won! He quickly hopped a train to D.C. and at a stop, someone handed him a newspaper and the title page read in big bold letters "Dewey defeats Truman!" He laughed and held it out for all to see. The famous picture of him holding that newspaper has been engraved in the brains of Americans everywhere. The people at the newspaper were so sure he was going to lose that they printed it on the cover page.

Ever watch a President speak on TV? It seems he always has a lot to say. A few years before Dwight David Eisenhower became President, he was President of Columbia University. He was at a dinner where several speakers got up to say something and they saved him for last. He surely was as tired as everyone else there listening to speech after speech, so when it was his turn, he got up and said, "I am the punctuation – the period," and sat down. I think there are many people who can learn from this, don't you?

Do you know what a negative ad is? Usually during an election year you see all these commercials on TV with someone running for office and all they do is talks bad about the person they are running against to get you to vote for *them* instead of the 'bad person.' Negative ads didn't start until the 1950s. Sure there were tons of it in magazines and newspapers, but never on TV. In 1956, there was a negative ad against Dwight Eisenhower, but the guy he was running against lost anyway. Shouldn't history teach us something about that? Can't we all just get along?

America is a country of traditions. Think about it. What do we do on July 4th? We celebrate the Independence of America. In January, we celebrate Martin Luther King Jr.'s birthday, in February we celebrate President's day, we have Labor Day, Arbor day, Veteran's Day… ok so what about Turkey Day? No I don't actually mean Thanksgiving Day – well I kind of do, but… there's a twist. Have you heard of Turkey Pardon Day? It isn't an official 'holiday,' but every year just before Thanksgiving, the President of the United States has a very important job. He gets to pardon (or release) a turkey from being cooked for Thanksgiving dinner. It's true. The first President to do it was Abraham Lincoln, but he didn't turn it into a tradition, he just did it. Later, President Truman was credited with doing it, but he actually didn't. The President who made it a tradition was George H.W. Bush (the father). He made it an official Presidential Act, so every President does it. Coincidentally, John F. Kennedy pardoned a turkey just three days before he was assassinated.

Ok, are you ready for another mystery detective case? The year is 1963, the place – Dallas, Texas, the time, about noon. The Presidential motorcade – a long line of limos and cars and police escorts - parade through downtown Dallas. President Kennedy is seated in an open car – no roof – with his wife seated next to him. As they turned on to Elm Street and proceeded into Dealey Plaza, tons of citizens were on the sidewalk and grass waving, cheering, taking pictures and screaming just to get a glimpse of the young Presidential couple. They were in the car with the Governor of Texas and his wife and she said, "You can't say that Dallas doesn't love you," and he responded, "You certainly can't." Then there was a shot and JFK lunged forward and said "My God! I'm hit!" What followed were more gun shots and he slumped over. Some people pointed up at a school book building behind them, but some pointed at an area just to the right of the motorcade where there were a bunch of bushes. The case went cold after that. The country was in mourning (this happened just before Thanksgiving). The police found a gunman who worked in the school book building, but the mystery about the grassy knoll area remained a mystery. Was there more than one gunman? Before Lee Harvey Oswald, the man accused of shooting the President, was taken to court, he was killed on live TV (the first time that *that* had ever happened), so they never really got his side of the story. He just kept saying that he was used, which made people think there was a conspiracy (meaning they think more than one person did this working together as a team). Even after a Committee that was put together by President Johnson came to believe that Oswald acted alone, there are still millions of Americans that believe there was more than one gunman. What do you think?

Here's a trick question. I covered the age of qualification to be President, but who was the youngest President of the United States? If you said John F. Kennedy, you're right… kind of.

John Fitzgerald Kennedy was the youngest *elected* President at 43 years of age, but Teddy Roosevelt was just weeks away from his 43rd birthday when he assumed office of the President, not by election, but because he was Vice President under President William McKinley and the President was killed. So technically, Teddy was the youngest President. The trick to this question is whether you use the word "*elected*" or not, remember that.

Speaking of age, Joe Biden was the oldest elected President; he was 78 years old. Second oldest was Donald Trump at 70 years 220 days. Ironically Joe was elected to office right after Donald, does that mean the next president will be in his 80's when elected?

Who was the oldest living President after leaving office? That honor went to George Herbert Walker Bush, who was President from 1989-1993. He passed Gerald Ford's record as oldest president. Ford died when he was 93, Bush passed away at 94. Jimmy Carter then passed them both when he turned 96 on October 1, 2020.

Do you have a big brother or sister? Are they the ones who get the most attention? We had a President who had to deal with that issue growing up, but because of it, he ended up in the White House. Joseph and Rose had a son named Joe Jr. He was the apple of his father's eyes. His dad had big plans for him, he was going to be President. Young Joe could do no wrong in his Dad's eyes. He was a star athlete in school, he joined the armed forces, and fought in the war. Everyone loved him. His younger brother fought for attention, but the younger brother, "Jack" as the family called him, was thin and sickly most of the time. He wasn't very athletic because he got sick a lot, but he loved to write. While in college, he wrote an essay that got him a lot of attention. His big brother was proud of him, but there was always that competition there. Well, the older brother was on a secret mission in the war... and he was killed. Joe didn't have his star son anymore and he was very sad, but then something happened out of it all, the second son quickly was groomed into the man that Joe wanted Junior to be, and "Jack" – or if you want to call him by his birth name – John, as in John F. Kennedy, worked his way up from second son to President of the United States.

Have you ever been in a TV studio? It's pretty neat. The lights, cameras, the crew hurrying around making sure everything is right just before the floor director counts off, 3-2-1. It's a pretty exciting place to be. Well one day a few years ago, the TV studio was very lively. It was a big deal, it was history being made. John and Richard were actually friends and they were going to be on TV together. They shook hands, joked about stuff. They had known each other at least twenty years before that day. They were dressed in suits, they memorized their lines, the staff made sure they were on cue. Millions of people were going to watch them. Wouldn't you be nervous? The director stepped out, it was time to start – was it a comedy show? A talk show? A reality show? Nope... it was the 1960 Presidential debates which would be televised for the first time in history and Richard Nixon faced off with his old friend John F. Kennedy on live TV.

    Back during World War II, the Navy had a fleet of PT Boats. PT stood for Patrol Torpedo and the amazing thing about them was they were light boats made mostly of plywood. During the war, a young lieutenant was in command of a PT boat and during the dead of night they got rammed by a huge Japanese ship out in the water in the middle of nowhere! The ship split in two and started to sink. The men on the PT109 swam for hours looking for land. They finally found a small island and were later rescued, but the lieutenant saved one of his men who was hurt, by grabbing the man's strap in his teeth and swimming for hours until they found the safety of the island. The young lieutenant became a hero and eventually the 35th President of the United States. His name was John F. Kennedy.

Here's an easy quiz. How many World Wars have we had? WWI was in the early part of the 1900s, WWII started in the late 1930s. But did we have a WWIII? The answer is "*No, but we almost did.*" Back in the fall of 1962, the United States and a country called the Soviet Union (Russia) weren't too fond of each other. Both were superpowers, meaning they both had nuclear weapons and could blow up a lot of stuff, including each other. After WWII ended, something called "The Cold War" began, meaning there was tension between the two countries, both knowing and fearing that the other would or could start another war. Russia decided to build missile sites in Cuba, a country just 90 miles south of Florida. President Kennedy thought that was a dangerous move to have Soviet missiles and bombs that close to us, so he issued a blockade, which sent American ships out to sea to block any Russian ship from passing and making it to Cuba. It was like a chess match that no one wanted to lose, but finally – days later – Kennedy and Soviet Premier Khrushchev came to an agreement and the world was saved from another possible World War.

Do you have brothers or sisters? They wouldn't happen to have the same first name initial as you, would they? Some parents like to do that, they'll have three kids and name one Jimmy, another Jeremy, and the girl Jennifer. It's common. Our 36th President went one better, Lyndon Baines Johnson, who liked to go by his initials LBJ, married a woman named Claudia Taylor, but her nickname was Lady Bird – also LBJ, they also had two daughters, Lynda Bird and Luci Baines – also LBJs and then they had a dog named… are you ready? Little Beagle Johnson. I wonder what they named the goldfish? What would you have named it?

First Ladies Moment:
Eleanor Roosevelt

Few women have held the title "First Lady" and could be remembered with as much respect as Eleanor Roosevelt. Before her, the wife of the President usually served as a "Hostess," they rarely got involved in the job of their husband, and dealing with public matters was out of the question. Eleanor changed that. She was very outspoken for human rights, children and women's issues – she considered herself a worker for the people. She even gave press conferences. She was so well sought after that when John F. Kennedy was running for President, he went to her and asked her to endorse him!

Chapter Nine:
Crisis Years, 1969-1993

Richard Nixon to George H.W. Bush

Impeachment is a bad word. Well, it's not a bad word that you can get in trouble for saying, but for a President it's a bad word. It means "we want to kick you out of office, we want to fire you." But you can't just fire a President; you have to have a really good reason. Andrew Johnson was someone they wanted to impeach because he had ideas after the Civil War that he thought would bring the country together, just like Lincoln had planned. Some people saw it another way. Then in the 1970s a Congressional Committee was working on plans to impeach Richard Nixon – they probably would have gone through with the full process had he not quit. Some men he knew broke into an office to get some secrets and they got caught. He said he didn't know anything about it, but it was later proven that he did know. It was the Watergate Scandal, and it was big news. Nixon, to get away from being impeached, did something no other President has *ever* done, he quit.

Bill Clinton was next in line for the dreaded "I" word. Some said he lied to the Congress while under oath (when you go to court and promise to tell the truth, and you lie – you can get in trouble for that). In the end he was acquitted (cleared).

The next impeachment didn't happen until the fall of 2019, but we'll talk about that later.

So, have you decided that you want to be President yet? Let's see if I can convince you. Imagine waking up in the morning and not ever having to make your own bed. No, someone else does that for you – and not just that – but you get fresh clean sheets. Then suppose you woke up in the morning and could pick up a phone and order whatever you wanted for breakfast. "Oh – today I'll have blueberry pancakes, eggs over easy, three pieces of toast with butter and grapefruit juice (don't go *ewww*, it's good for you!)" And then tomorrow morning, "A bowl of Fruit Loops with milk, a strawberry muffin and a banana." Whatever you want, it's made for you and even brought to your room if you want. You get someone to drive you around wherever you want to go – and they don't bother you about your homework. You get your own plane and helicopter. But, your days are full of important phone calls, meetings, speeches, and shaking hands. I don't know about you but I could deal with shaking hands as long as I could get French toast and orange juice every morning!

Ok so let's go back to the rules. To become President, you have to be *elected* to the office, right? Right. So every person that has held the office of President – aside from those that moved up from Vice-President after the President died in office – was there because he was elected, right? Right, *well...* except for one man. During the 1970s, Richard Nixon had to deal with the matter of his Vice-President's resignation. When Vice-President Spiro Agnew resigned, Nixon appointed Gerald Ford as Vice-President. Then the Watergate controversy caused Richard Nixon to resign (we covered that, remember?). So, Gerald Ford became the only man in history to become Vice-President and later President of the United States without being elected. Geez, talk about being in the right place at the right time!

Whenever you see the President somewhere, he's always followed by men dressed in black suits. Who are they? No it isn't Will Smith and Agent K looking for aliens. It's the Secret Service, and they're whole job is to defend and protect the President, right? Well kind of. They spend a lot of their time doing that now, but back

in 1865 when they were formed, they had one job, to detect and suppress counterfeiting. Yep they had to follow fake money and catch the criminals that were making it. I think it's kind of funny, some agents follow the Presidents and some agents follow the *pictures* of Presidents on green paper!

Has anyone in your family ever made a long distance call? Where's the farthest place they called? Canada? Puerto Rico? China? Australia? What do you think is the farthest place you can make a long distance call to? Well, with today's technology you can pick up a cell phone and call anywhere (just don't do it without asking for permission – it's important!), but back in 1969, technology wasn't anywhere near what it is today. Yet one man called the farthest place you can imagine... the moon! In July of that year, Buzz Aldrin (That's where Buzz Lightyear got his first name) and Neil Armstrong were on the moon, and they received a phone call from earth! Who was on the phone? President Richard Nixon. He will go down in the history books as the President who made the first phone call to the moon. I'm going to make a guess that by the time *you* get to the White House, you will be the first President to call Mars!

Do you know what hospital you were born in? Most people do because everyone was born in a hospital, right? Well, wrong. The first President to be born in a hospital was Jimmy Carter, and he was President back in the 1970s. So where were all the other Presidents before him born? Usually at home. Back in the day, instead of going to a hospital, there was a nurse, called a midwife, and her job was to deliver babies. She would travel from house to house and deliver the newborns. Can you imagine being a midwife and not knowing until years later that the baby you helped bring into the world would end up becoming President of the United States?

Sometimes being serious all the time isn't a good thing. Jimmy Carter wasn't known for his humor. Though people close to him said he did have a funny side to him, he just didn't show it in public. Jimmy rose from peanut farmer, to Naval Officer to State Senator, to Governor of Georgia. When all that was done, he turned to his mother one day, he was fifty years old, and said, "Mom, I'm going to run for President." She turned to him and replied, "President of what?"

Can you imagine a famous movie star like say Johnny Depp, becoming President? Sounds far-fetched huh? But something like that actually happened. Ronald Reagan was a movie star from the late 1930s all the way to the 1960s. He was a very well-liked actor, just like Johnny Depp. One of the roles that really made Ronald Reagan a household name was when he played the team star of coach Knute Rockne's football team (Knute was a football player and later coach at Notre Dame in the early 20th Century – in fact he was in college when the Titanic went down). In the movie, Reagan's name was George Gipp. In a memorable scene when he's in the hospital he asks his coach to tell the team to "win one for the Gipper". This phrase is still famous and often used today.

What's the most embarrassing thing that's ever happened to you at the dinner table? Spilled milk on your Grandma? Burped after a big salad? Maybe laughed so hard that Capri-Sun ran down your nose during Thanksgiving? Whatever it was, it *can't* be as bad as what happened to George H.W. Bush. As you know, we had two Presidents named Bush. One is the father of the other. George H.W. is the father. He was on an important trip to Japan and was at a big dinner, I mean this diner was bigger than Thanksgiving! He was surrounded by important people and he… well, *he threw up* on a Japanese diplomat – a very important person. Can you top that? Wait, please don't try.

You've probably seen pictures of a lot of our Presidents. If you could pick one that you thought was a model when he was younger which would you pick? Hmm, let's see, John F. Kennedy was handsome, or Barak Obama, or Bill Clinton? How about Gerald Ford? Well believe it or not, when Ford was in law school, he made extra money by modeling. He was even on the cover of Cosmopolitan magazine! I guess you can say he was a *model* of a good President.

Do you like spinach? It wasn't one of my favorites growing up, but I'll eat it now if it's cooked with chicken or something. That happens to a lot of people, you may like one thing growing up, then not like it later. Chocolate milk, cheese, bananas… how about broccoli? Well, we had one President who didn't like broccoli; I mean he *really* didn't like it. When asked about it once, George H.W. Bush was serious in his reply "I don't like broccoli, my mom made me eat it when I was little and I don't like it! I'm President of the United States and I will not eat broccoli!"

He might have thought broccoli would kill him as a youngster, but Bush really had a near death experience over the ocean when back during World War II, his plane was shot by the enemy and he was forced to eject and land in the water. He was on a bombing mission and when his plane was hit, he landed in the Pacific and floated for four hours before a submarine crew pulled him out of the water. He received several citations during the war for being a hero. This happened in 1944, the same year that Franklin Roosevelt announced that he would run for a fourth term!

First Lady Moment:
Rosalynn Carter

Born in the same town as her husband, Eleanor Rosalynn Smith liked to use her middle name instead of her first name. She worked at a hairdresser's shop in her younger days, but after Jimmy Carter became President, she was the *first* First Lady to have her own office in the East Wing. Rosalynn was a very active participant in the day to day job of her husband. She attended meetings, traveled and spoke with dignitaries, and even consulted with the President about his decisions in office. She supported equal rights and was very vocal on controversial issues.

Chapter Ten:
New Millenia, 1993-Present

Bill Clinton to Joe Biden

Ever got a *D* on your report card? Getting a *D* isn't supposed to be a good thing, but it was for one little boy. You see, he was very smart in class, he always got *A*s. Then he brought his report card home and showed it to his Mom. She looked at it, and there was a *D* for conduct. She had to look again, a *D!* There had to be something wrong, she knew her little Billy was one of the smartest kids in class! She called the teacher, she had to know. Maybe she put the *D* on the wrong kid's report card? Yeah, that *had* to be it! But she later found out that the *D* was there and it was meant for her son, but not for the reason she thought. She gave him a *D* in conduct, she said, because he was so smart and so competitive that she thought he would struggle harder in school to overcome the grade. She was right, her son Billy – Bill Clinton went on to become a Rhodes Scholar, which is a very high honor and prestigious award for any student.

Earlier you read where Sara Knox Taylor, daughter of Zachary (who was still years away from becoming President), married Jefferson Davis – who would later become President of the Confederacy. Could there possibly be another marriage between Presidents in American History? Why of course there was, this milestone happened when the daughter of Richard Nixon, Julie, married the grandson of President Eisenhower, David, in 1968. They met in 1956 when they were both eight years old!

The Presidents are all images in history to most of us. Usually at one time or another there might be two or three past Presidents still alive at the same time, but is there a place you can see *all* of the United States Presidents together in one spot? Yes. But you'll have to pack up the family and come to Walt Disney World in Florida. Visiting the Hall of Presidents (my favorite attraction in the Magic Kingdom) is like sitting in an elaborate auditorium where *all* of the U.S. Presidents sit or stand. Disney's creative imagineers have developed an incredible stage show where you are introduced to each President, and then some of them speak. I can tell you that as a ten year old who was taken there for the first time, it sealed my admiration for my love of all things Presidential. If you haven't been to it, or thought it might be boring, next time you go to Walt Disney World you have to see it. You won't be disappointed. By the way, this isn't a paid announcement. ☺

You've heard of Air Force One, right? No, not the shoes, the plane. Well it isn't just any plane. Technically, Air Force One is the name of *any* plane that the President is on. So yes, it doesn't have to be the actual one that he normally travels in. If he landed in Tampa, Florida, then took his motorcade (a bunch of his cars that take him and his staff from one place to another) to Lakeland, Florida and something came up and he had to be flown back to Washington D.C. in a hurry, he could catch a ride on Billy-Bob's Crop Duster Service and be flown to the nation's capital. The whole time he's on that plane it would be called Air Force One. Of course Billy Bob's plane would be nothing in comparison to the plane we all refer to as Air Force One. That plane has three levels, an office for the President, a bedroom, six guest bathrooms, a dining room… geez all he needs is a movie theater in there!

In 2016, Hillary Clinton finally accomplished something that no other woman was able to do. She made it all the way through the primary elections (where people vote for POTUS) and almost got elected President. This was one of those times where what the people voted and what the electoral college (The elected officials who cast the winning vote), differed. She won the people's vote but he won the electoral college vote – so he won. But it wouldn't take long for another woman to finally make it to the White House, though not as President. In 2020 Kamala Harris, a Senator from California, was chosen by Joe Biden to be his Vice President. It took a few (200 plus) years to get there, but she did it. You know what that means right? If you're a girl, nothing is stopping you from becoming President one day – I'll vote for you.

Do you like sports? How about football? Several Presidents had a past in football, including Nixon, Kennedy, Ford, Eisenhower, Reagan… and Trump? Ok, well "The Donald" didn't actually play the sport, but in 1982 when the United States Football League, a new league with new teams started, he owned the New Jersey Generals, but he later sold them. The league didn't last long. By 1985 the USFL had phased out.

The President has many titles. One of them is Commander-In-Chief. As Commander-In-Chief, the President is the top person of every branch of military in the United States. Whenever a soldier, officer, or any enlisted man or woman in our military is in presence of the President, they have to salute, and he has to salute back. Think about that for a second, if you're the President and you are taken to a military base, can you imagine how many times you'd have to lift your arm to salute back?

There have been many children in and out of the White House, but were there ever any twins in the Executive Mansion? Well, the answer would be yes, and do you know which President was the father of the *first* First Twins? George W. and Laura Bush had twins Barbara and Jenna – both named after their grandmothers.

Pennsylvania is known for a few things: the Liberty Bell, Benjamin Franklin, Hershey Park. But how many Presidents came from the Keystone State? That would be two... James Buchanan, who was born in Cove Gap in 1791 (he was eight years old when George Washington died) and he was also the president who served before Lincoln. The state of Pennsylvania would have to wait all the way until 1942 for the next one, that's when Joe Biden's parents brought home their new son.

Barak Obama has a distinction as being the first President for something that no other President can claim, do you know what it is? Well, ok, that's a trick question because the first response would be "the *first* African-American President," and you'd be right, but he also has another distinction that no other President before him can claim. Give up? He was the first President to be born outside of the continental United States. Of our 50 states, two of them aren't connected to each other on the North American continent – or as we call them, "the lower 48." Alaska, up north, is connected to Canada, and President Obama's place of birth – Hawaii – is out in the Pacific Ocean. There was a big move during his first term to prove that he was born in Hawaii and he later presented his birth certificate to prove that he was. Do you know why they insisted on making sure he was born in the United States.? Do you remember, back in chapter one – one of the rules of being President?

In 1963 President Kennedy introduced the Presidential Medal of Freedom, the highest civilian honor that a president can give to a person. To date, only three Vice-Presidents have had the honor to receive one; Nelson Rockefeller, Hubert Humphrey, and Joe Biden. Of the three, only one managed to step into the Oval office as President – Joe Biden.

Ever watch the Grammys? It's where recording artists get major props for being good at what they do. Can you imagine a President getting a Grammy? Well, believe it or not, three have, all for spoken recordings of books. Bill Clinton won a Grammy in 2004 for his voice narrating the English version of *Wolf Track*. Then he won a Grammy in 2005 with his autobiography *My Life*. Jimmy Carter won a Grammy for *Our Endangered Value: America's Moral Crisis*. Barack Obama won two, one for *Dreams from My Father* in 2006, and the other for *The Audacity of Hope* in 2008.

Ronald Reagan was known as a radio, then movie star before he ever got into politics. Most people in Hollywood wouldn't even consider a career in government, but another famous TV star also made it to the White House. In 2004, a new Reality TV show aired for the first time. It was called "The Apprentice" and it's star, Donald Trump, later became President.

On September 11th, 2001, in the morning when most of us were either in school, at work, or eating breakfast at home, a commercial airplane crashed into one of the Twin Towers in New York City. The twin towers were two skyscrapers that stood in Manhattan and were an emblem of American pride. Terrorists carefully planned an attack on the United States and this started a war on terror that the United States decided to make a priority. The world expected a quick response from the POTUS (President of the Unites States), but he wasn't in the White House. Where was he?

That morning, President George W. Bush was actually at an elementary school in Florida reading with some kids. But he was soon back in the oval office taking care of business.

We've had a good number of Presidents so far and you'd think that with fifty states we'd have covered almost each state at least once as far as Presidential birthplaces go, but here is the list of states where a President has *NOT* been born in yet: Alabama, Alaska, Arizona, Colorado, Delaware, Florida, Idaho, Indiana, Kansas, Louisiana, Maine, Maryland, Michigan, Minnesota, Mississippi, Montana, Nevada, New Mexico, North Dakota, Oklahoma, Oregon, Rhode Island, South Dakota, Tennessee, Utah, Washington, West Virginia, Wisconsin, and Wyoming. Ok, if you live in one of these states, we need you in the White House so we can scratch your state off the list!

Are you good at math? Ok let's figure this out. When you get a job, you get paid to work. So let's say your mom is paid $60,000 a year salary ("salary" is what you get paid to work). You don't get paid in a year you usually get paid every week or every two weeks. So let's break this down. At 60 thousand dollar salary broken down into 12 months means that your mom makes $5,000 a month because 5 x 12 = 60, right? Ok so if you broke that down into weeks at four weeks in a month, she'd bring home $1,250 a week. That's not bad; you could buy a lot of candy with that. So when George Washington started, do you remember what his salary was? $25,000 a year. As we have read earlier, the Presidential salary has grown over the years, from $25,000 to 50, then 75, then 100, then 200, and now 400 thousand a year. That's what President Trump makes, although he has chosen to donate his salary back to the government. Ironically, when he was starring in the TV show *The Apprentice*, he was making almost that for EVERY show. He was paid $375,000 for every episode. Why do you think they pay TV and movie stars more than the President?

So, remember the dreaded "I" word from chapters before? You get ten points and a peanut butter sandwich if you can remember the word. Ok, wait, there are no points, and I ate the peanut butter sandwich – anyway, the word is *impeach*. Well, in the fall of 2019, another President faced the dreaded act of impeachment. This time it was President Trump. What was the accusation? I'm glad you asked. He was accused of trying to get the president of another country to dig up information on an ex-vice president, who just happened to be in the running for office for the 2020 elections. The ex-vice-president's son had worked for a company in that country while his father was in office. Some said that it was illegal for the President of the United States to do this, but President Trump was acquitted by the Senate. Then, on Wednesday, January 6, 2021, there was a rally in Washington, and some accused him of getting those in the audience to storm or raid the capitol building. But wait, *that's not all* – President Trump was impeached again will go down in history as the ONLY American President to be impeached twice. Yes, that's two times for the kid in the back row. Again, he was acquitted.

You see, the way impeachment works is that the House of Representatives has the power to impeach the President – that is to accuse him of wrongdoing, but it is the job of the Senate to decide the case – like a jury in a court.

So you would think that being President of the United States is a pretty cool job, huh? Well some of the men who held that job might disagree with you. Listen to what they said:

Lyndon Johnson: "The presidency has made every man who occupied it, no matter how small, bigger than he was; and no matter how big, not big enough for its demands."

Rutherford B. Hayes: "No one has ever left the Presidency with less regret than I do."

James Garfield: "...what is it about this place that a man should ever want to get here?"

Harry S Truman: "All the President is, is a glorified public relations man who spends his time flattering, kissing, and kicking people to get them to do what they are supposed to do anyway."

John Quincy Adams: "As to the Presidency, the two happiest days of my life were those of my entrance upon the office and my surrender of it."

James K. Polk: "With me it is exceptionally true that the Presidency is no bed of roses."

Zachary Taylor: "The idea that I should become President seems to me too visionary to require a serious answer. It has never entered my head, nor is it likely to enter the head of any other person."

Do you have the same birthday as a famous person? Have you ever looked to find out? It's easy on the internet. I share a birthday (different years of course) with Jennifer Lopez and Amelia Earhart. Well President Joe Biden shares his November 20th birthday with Robert F. Kennedy (1925), actress Bo Derek (1956), and Joe Walsh (1947).

Here are some other Presidential coincidences:

- The twenty-ninth President, Warren G. Harding, was born the year that President Lincoln was assassinated.

- Lincoln and Kennedy died in a place where the first and last names started with a *P* and an *H*. Kennedy in *P*arkland Memorial *H*ospital and Lincoln in the *P*eterson Boarding *H*ouse. Both were officially pronounced dead in the presence of doctors.

- At a train station, a young man fell and could have been killed but was saved by another man who grabbed his collar and pulled him to safety. The man who almost got killed was Robert Lincoln, son of Abraham. But the man who saved him was - Edwin Booth - brother to John Wilkes, who later killed Abraham.

- It doesn't end there with Robert Lincoln. After his father died, he was asked later by President Garfield to take a Cabinet position. At a gathering, he was invited to attend with the President, he arrived just in time to see Garfield get shot. But wait - that's not all! Years later, he was invited by President McKinley to the Pan Am Expo, which was like a fair. He got there - again just in time - to watch McKinley get assassinated. He quit government life after that.

- Some people have reported seeing the ghost of Abraham Lincoln in the White House, and I don't mean visitors like you and I. The wives of Presidents Coolidge and Lyndon Johnson, and even British Prime Minister Winston Churchill have all laid claim to this. Maybe he's looking for his hat?

- James Madison - our fourth President was second cousin to Zachary Taylor - our twelfth President.

- Abraham Lincoln is the first President to have his picture taken during an inauguration. It's a wide panorama shot with a lot of people in it all around him. Coincidentally, his assassin John Wilkes Booth is also in the photo.

In the beginning of this book, I made a time-line of how a former President met with a future yet unknown at the time President. Well folks, I want to share one more with you, you gotta love this history stuff:

- George Washington was the General of the Continental Army during the Revolutionary War. After America won her freedom, he signed the Declaration of Independence with several other men, among them, his friend Benjamin Harrison.

- Benjamin's son, William Henry Harrison, became President in 1841 and had many grandkids that lived and played on his huge estate. Among them, was little Benjamin Harrison.

- Benjamin Harrison was voted President in 1888, but served one term. After his White House duties were over, Harrison taught for a stint at Sanford University in California, where a young man from Ohio was studying geology, that man was future President Herbert Hoover.

- After the 1960 Presidential elections were over and Richard Nixon lost to John F. Kennedy, Nixon received a phone call from ex-President Hoover (through the urging of Kennedy's Dad – who was a friend) to meet with JFK for a chat. He did.

- President Nixon approved of and encouraged a date between his daughter Trish and a young man who was the son of a political friend. They dated secretly, but soon parted ways. That young man's name was George W. Bush.

- As President, George W. Bush gave his annual State of the Union Address – a speech he makes that is caught live on TV, the internet, and radio in which he shares his views and reports to the joint houses of Congress and the American people. In 2005, a newly elected Senator from Chicago was in chambers as Bush spoke, his name is Barak Obama.

There isn't a Presidential History *or* an American History book that I've seen that doesn't include the weird similarities between John F. Kennedy and Abraham Lincoln, so I'm going to follow suit and ask, ***did you know***:

- Kennedy and Lincoln were both assassinated by a shot to the head?

- Their assassins were known by their first, middle, and last names?

- That Kennedy had a secretary named Lincoln and Lincoln had a secretary named John?

- That both of them had Vice-Presidents who were Southerners and whose last name was Johnson? Plus, both Johnson's first names were 6 letters long? Plus, they were born a hundred years apart, 1808 and 1908.

- That their assassins were both killed before making it to trial?

- That they were elected President 100 years apart, 1860 and 1960.

- That they both had a son that died while they were in office?

- That both the assassin's names were 15 letters long?

- That both Presidents were avid readers.

- That both Presidents are considered the funniest of all? They both were great at making people laugh.

- That they both made similar comments about being killed before they were shot? "If someone wanted to shoot me, it would be easy to do." (paraphrased)

- That both men were assassinated sitting next to their wives.

- Lincoln was shot in Ford's Theater; Kennedy was shot while he was sitting in a Lincoln limousine (that was made by the Ford Motor company).

- Both Presidents were shot on a Friday.

- Both Presidents had strong concerns about civil rights.

- Booth shot Lincoln in a theater then ran to a warehouse; Oswald shot Kennedy from a warehouse and ran to a theater (where he later shot a policeman).

That's just crazy, huh??

First Lady Moment:
Michelle Obama

Michelle Robinson – or "Meesh" as her family calls her, met her husband while they worked in a law firm. It wasn't a sure thing that they would end up together, but Barak wouldn't quit. He thought she was one of the most beautiful women he had ever seen. She was devoted to women's and children's causes, and a strong supporter of families. Though she made sure she was a strong mother presence to her daughters, Michelle also worked alongside her husband on matters pertaining to his job. She was a very busy woman. Her big push on health in our country was criticized by some, but embraced by many.

Chapter Eleven
Hail to the Chief

Well, wasn't that a fun ride? We got to know a little more about the men, women, and children who occupied the White House. But wait, we're not done. Do you know what song is played for the President at official events? If you guessed, "Hail to the Chief" you'd be right. Now there's a test. Yes, a test, I told you there would be, remember? Don't worry, you can't fail this test because there are no points involved, but if you get all of the answers right then maybe someday a military band will be playing "Hail to the Chief for you! So, put on your thinking caps and let's see how much you remembered. *(Answers are at the end of the book – don't cheat!)*

1. Lyndon Baines Johnson and his whole family went by the initials LBJ, what did the LB stand for in his wife's name?

2. Who was the youngest President?

3. Ronald Reagan, George W. Bush and Franklin Roosevelt were all on teams in college, but it wasn't football, they were
    _____.

4. Sarah Taylor, daughter of President Zachary Taylor, married another President. He was President of _____.

5. Richard Nixon and Harry Truman were musicians, they played
    _____.

6. What did Harry S Truman's middle name stand for?

7. President _____ was afraid of electricity.

8. Teddy bears were named after which President?

9. Which President has the most places named after him?

10. Who did Bill Clinton meet when he was a boy?

11. Which President died on the 4th of July, the same day his friend John Adams did?

12. Which President had the most children?

13. President Hayes' wife refused to allow alcohol in the White House, so she got the nickname "_____ Lucy."

14. "Tecumseh's Curse" was broken when which President didn't die from an assassination attempt?

15. President Grant's name was changed when he entered West Point. His initials changed to U.S.G., which was ok with him. It was better than the initials he was born with, which were _ _ _.

16. President Calvin Coolidge was known for not talking so much, what was his nickname?

17. Richard Nixon made a long distance call to where?

18. Franklin Pierce was a sad President, his son died at the age of eleven on a _____.

19. What did U.S. Grant write before he died?

20. Name one of the four presidents in this book that were impeached or got this close to it.

Presidents' Roll Call

President	Party	Dates in Office
1. George Washington		1789–1797
2. John Adams	Federalist	1797–1801
3. Thomas Jefferson	Democratic-Republican	1801–1809
4. James Madison	Democratic-Republican	1809–1817
5. James Monroe	Democratic-Republican	1817–1825
6. John Q. Adams	Democratic-Republican	1825–1829
7. Andrew Jackson	Democratic	1829–1837
8. Martin Van Buren	Democratic	1837–1841
9. William H. Harrison	Whig	1841
10. John Tyler	Whig	1841–1845
11. James K. Polk	Democratic	1845–1849
12. Zachary Taylor	Whig	1849–1850

13. Millard Fillmore	Whig	1850–1853
14. Franklin Pierce	Democratic	1853–1857
15. James Buchanan	Democratic	1857–1861
16. Abraham Lincoln	Republican	1861–1865
17. Andrew Johnson	Democratic/National Union	1865–1869
18. Ulysses S. Grant	Republican	1869–1877
19. Rutherford B. Hayes	Republican	1877–1881
20. James Garfield	Republican	1881
21. Chester A. Arthur	Republican	1881–1885
22. Grover Cleveland	Democratic	1885–1889
23. Benjamin Harrison	Republican	1889–1893
24. Grover Cleveland	Democratic	1893–1897
25. William McKinley	Republican	1897–1901
26. Theodore Roosevelt	Republican	1901–1909
27. William Howard Taft	Republican	1909–1913
28. Woodrow Wilson	Democratic	1913–1921
29. Warren G. Harding	Republican	1921–1923
30. Calvin Coolidge	Republican	1923–1929

31. Herbert Hoover	Republican	1929–1933
32. Franklin D. Roosevelt	Democratic	1933–1945
33. Harry S Truman	Democratic	1945–1953
34. Dwight D. Eisenhower	Republican	1953–1961
35. John F. Kennedy	Democratic	1961–1963
36. Lyndon B. Johnson	Democratic	1963–1969
37. Richard M. Nixon	Republican	1969–1974
38. Gerald R. Ford	Republican	1974–1977
39. James E. Carter	Democratic	1977–1981
40. Ronald W. Reagan	Republican	1981–1989
41. George H. W. Bush	Republican	1989–1993
42. William J. Clinton	Democratic	1993–2001
43. George W. Bush	Republican	2001–2009
44. Barack Obama	Democratic	2009–2017
45. Donald J. Trump	Republican	2017-2021
46. Joseph R. Biden	Democratic	2021-

Bibliography:

Boller, Paul F. *Presidential Anecdotes*. New York: Oxford University Press, 1996.

Boller, Paul F. *Presidential Campaigns*. New York: Oxford University Press, 1984.

Boller, Paul F. *Presidential Wives: An Anecdotal History*. New York: Oxford University Press, 1988.

Davis, Kenneth C. *Don't Know Much About American History*. New York: HarperCollins. 2003.

Davis, Kenneth C. *Don't Know Much About The Presidents*. Harper Collins, 2002.

Gomez, Rebecca. *Quick Quizzes: Presidents*. New York: Kids books, 2004.

Johnson, David E. & Johnny R. Johnson. *A Funny Thing Happened on The Way To The White House*. New York: Barnes & Noble, 2007.

Krull, Kathleen. *Lives of The Presidents*. New York, Harcourt, Brace & Co. 1998

Lengyel, Cornel Adam. Presidents of the United States. New York: Golden Press, 1970.

O'Reilly, Bill and Martin Dugard. *Killing Lincoln*. New York: Henry Holt, 2011

Pine, Joslyn (editor). *Presidential Wit & Wisdom*. New York: Dover Publications, 2009

Ridings, Jr., William J. & Stuart B. McIver. *Rating The Presidents*. Secaucus, NJ: Citadel Press, 1997

Sandler, Martin. *Presidents: A Library of Congress Book*. New York: Harper Collins, 1995

Smith, Carter. *Presidents: Every Question Answered*. New York: Metro Books, 2008.

Stebben, Gregory, *White House Confidential*. Nashville: Cumberland House Pub., 1998

Sullivan, George. *Facts and Fun About The Presidents*. New York: Scholastic, 1987

Uncle John's Bathroom Reader Plunges Into The Presidency. San Diego: Portable Press, 2004

Williams, Stephen. *How To Be President*. San Francisco: Chronicle Books, 2004

Whitney, David C. & Robin V. Whitney. *The American Presidents*. New York: Guild America Books (Bookspan), 2001

Answer Key

(from pages 86-87)

1. *Lady Bird*

2. *Theodore "Teddy" Roosevelt (I didn't say "elected")*

3. *Cheerleaders*

4. *The Confederacy*

5. *Piano*

6. *Nothing*

7. *Benjamin Harrison*

8. *Teddy Roosevelt*

9. *Washington*

10. *John F. Kennedy*

11. *Thomas Jefferson*

12. *John Tyler*

13. *Lemonade*

14. *Reagan*

15. *H.U.G.*

16. *Silent Cal*

17. *The moon.*

18. *train*

19. *His Memoirs (Life Story)*

20. *Johnson, Nixon, Clinton, Trump*

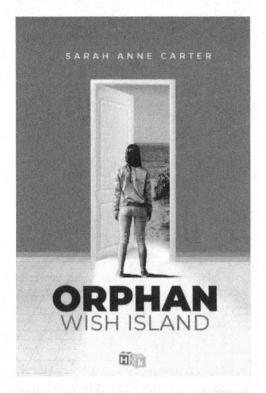